This Bible is a special gift to:

_____

With love from:

_____

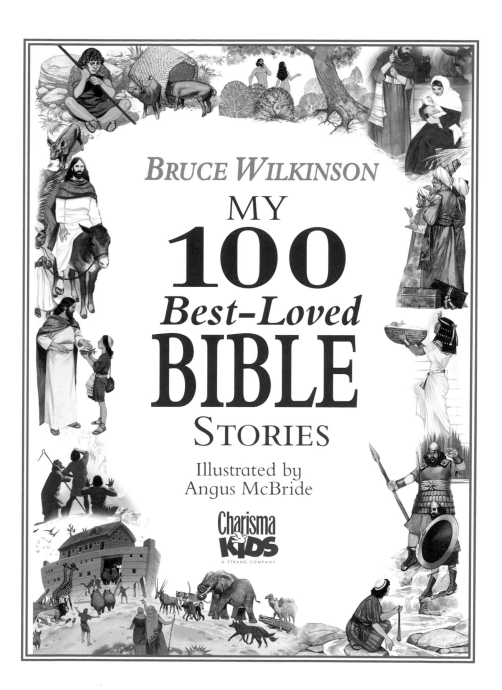

BRUCE WILKINSON

MY
100
Best-Loved
BIBLE
STORIES

Illustrated by
Angus McBride

Charisma
KIDS
A STRANG COMPANY

My 100 Best-Loved Bible Stories
by Bruce Wilkinson

Requests for information may be addressed to:

The children's book imprint of Strang Communications Company
600 Rinehart Rd., Lake Mary, FL 32746
www.charismakids.com

Designed by Brenda Smal

Library of Congress Control Number 2005926712
International Standard Book Number 1-59185-866-6

05 06 07 08 09 – 987654321
Printed in China

A Special Word to Parents

My 100 Best-Loved Bible Stories is not an ordinary storybook, but a book that wants to convey the **good news** that God dearly loves each of your little ones.

Not only does it tell the intriguing stories of people who lived long ago, but it also reveals the secret of the living God who speaks to us today through the lives of these Bible characters. When the little ones learn about God's love for His people and the special way He cares for them, they will be inspired to find out more about God and how to serve Him.

This book does not only want to tell wonderful stories. It also wants to draw your child into the world of the Bible. Enjoy the way your child becomes part of the surprises awaiting God's people, and share in the adventure of Jesus' friends. Listen with your child how the story of the Bible unfolds:

❖ First the **Old Testament** where God's plan with the world from its beginning and His commitment to His people in good and bad times are revealed.

❖ Then the **New Testament** where God enters into a new covenant with His people through Jesus who lives in us.

Reading *My 100 Best-Loved Bible Stories* will be an exciting adventure during which both you and your child will learn to know God better. At the end of each story the little ones get the chance to open their hearts before God in **prayer** and to show their love for Him.

The **chat box** is to help them become actively involved in the Bible story and to do something special to remember the message of the story.

Some of the **difficult words** in the stories are printed in bold. Right at the back of the book these words are explained to the little ones in a way they will understand.

In This Bible

Old
Testament

God has a great plan for the world and all His people

We learn to know God our Father.
God made everything, and He is always with
His people. God loves His people. God cares
for His children like a father, even if they
don't always love Him. God gives His people
a new country to live in. He promises that He
will make them happy.

1. God Made the World

Who made this beautiful world?
  It was our great God.
  Everything was cold and dark.
  No one likes the dark.
  So, God made light.
  God gave us the sun for daytime.
  God also gave us the moon and the stars
  for nighttime.
God made the sea…and the dry land.
  He made the plants as well…the flowers with
  their pretty colors, and all the different trees.

Genesis 1

God our Father, how great You are! Thank You for
everything You've made. Amen.

CHAT BOX
Look through the window. What do you see?
Who made it all? God did!

2. God Made the Animals and the People

Our great God also made many other things in this beautiful world of ours.

He made the fish that swim in the water. He also made the birds that sing so beautifully.

God made animals: wild animals and tame animals…even the small creatures and the bugs.

Then God made something very special…people. He loves them dearly!

The first people He made were Adam and Eve.

Genesis 1

God our Father, thank You that You have made everything so beautiful. Amen.

Point with your finger to the things God made. Tell us what they are. Can you think of any other things God made?

3. A Garden of Great Beauty

Look at this beautiful garden. This garden is called Eden.

God tells Adam and Eve they may live here. All they have to do is to take care of the garden.

God says, "Listen carefully. Don't eat from this one tree!" It is the tree in the middle of the garden.

The bad **devil** lies to Eve, "You don't have to listen to God!" The fruit looks delicious. Eve and Adam eat of it.

God is very sad. Adam and Eve know they have done wrong.

Now they have to leave this beautiful garden.

Genesis 2; 3:1-7

God our Father, please help me to always listen to You. Amen.

CHAT ⌐BOX

*What did you learn? The **devil** always tells lies. We will rather listen to God, because we love Him.*

4. Noah's Big Ship

Do you see Noah? He loves God very much.
God says, "Noah, there will be a huge flood.
The whole earth will be covered with water."

Noah has to build an ark. It is a very big ship. Noah and his family have to get inside the ark.

And animals also have to go inside—one male and one female of every kind.

Then the rain started. It rained day after day until all the land on earth was under water.

But Noah, his family, and the animals were safe inside the ark.

Genesis 6–7

God our Father, thank You that we are always safe with You. Amen.

CHAT BOX

Point with your finger to Noah and his family. Let's see if you know the names of the animals in the picture. Which of the animals do you like best?

5. The Many Colors of the Rainbow

God promised Noah that if he listened to Him,
He would save Noah and his family and all the
animals in the ark.

God promised. And then He did what He had
promised. That is how God is.

God sent a strong wind. The wind blew the water
away. The earth was dry again. Noah and his family
could get safely out of the ark again.

God promised Noah, "The earth will never again be
covered by water."

Then they saw a beautiful rainbow. It is God's sign
that He will keep His promise.

Genesis 8-9

God our Father, thank You that You always do as You promise. Amen.

6. The People Build a Tower

There are now many people on the earth. God wants them to live in one place, but they don't listen to Him. They start building a very high tower to show how clever they are. They all speak the same language. They like working together.

But then God makes the people speak in different languages. One asks, "What are you saying?" The other says, "I don't understand you." Now they don't want to live together anymore.

From then on the people lived all over the whole world.

Genesis 11

God our Father, please help me to believe that You always know best. Amen.

CHAT BOX
Point to the tower. Ask mom or dad to show you a map of the world. See how people live all over the world.

7. Abraham Moves to a Faraway Land

Long ago there was a man named Abraham. God told Abraham to move to a faraway country.

Abraham, his wife, Sarah, and his nephew Lot all moved away together. They lived happily in the new country.

But then Abraham's and Lot's workers started fighting. Abraham was unhappy. He said to Lot, "Choose where you want to live." Lot chose the best place. It had the most beautiful plants and streams.

But God promised Abraham that he would have many children. God would take care of them.

Genesis 12–13

God our Father, thank You that You also take care of me.
Amen.

┌─**BOX**
CHAT *Point to where Lot chose to stay.*
Where did Abraham go?
Who promised to take care of Abraham?

8. Sarah Doubts God

God promised Abraham that he would have many children. But now Abraham and Sarah are very old. And still they have no children.

One day three men come to visit Abraham. They tell him that Sarah will have a son. Sarah hears it and laughs.

God asks, "Why are you laughing? Don't you believe that I can do what I promised?"

Later they have a boy. They call him Isaac. They thank God for him.

Genesis 18, 21

God our Father, thank You that You always do what You promise to do. Amen.

CHAT BOX How does Sarah's face look? What did you learn? God can do things people cannot do. Look at the picture. Can you meow like a cat?

9. Isaac Gets a Beautiful Wife

Abraham's son Isaac is now a young man. So Abraham sends his servant Eliezer to find him a wife.

The servant asks, "How will I know who is the right woman?"

Abraham answers, "The Lord will show you."

Eliezer rests at a well where the young women come to draw water. When Rebecca arrives,

God shows Eliezer that she will become Isaac's wife.

Genesis 24

God our Father, thank You that You help us to love each other. Amen.

10. Jacob Has to Run Away

Isaac and Rebecca have two sons. Esau is the oldest. Jacob is the youngest. They do not look alike at all. Esau's skin is hairy. Jacob's skin is smooth.

Jacob wants Esau's special gift.

Isaac, their father, is very old. He can't see well anymore. Rebecca, their mother, covers Jacob's arms with the skin of a goat. Isaac feels the hairy skin. He thinks it is Esau. He gives Esau's special gift to Jacob!

Esau is very angry with Jacob. Jacob has to run away from home as fast as he can.

Genesis 27

God our Father, please help me to love my family. Amen.

⌐BOX
CHAT *What is Jacob doing? His brother Esau is not there. He went
to shoot a buck for his father. Can you show how to shoot
with a bow and arrow?*

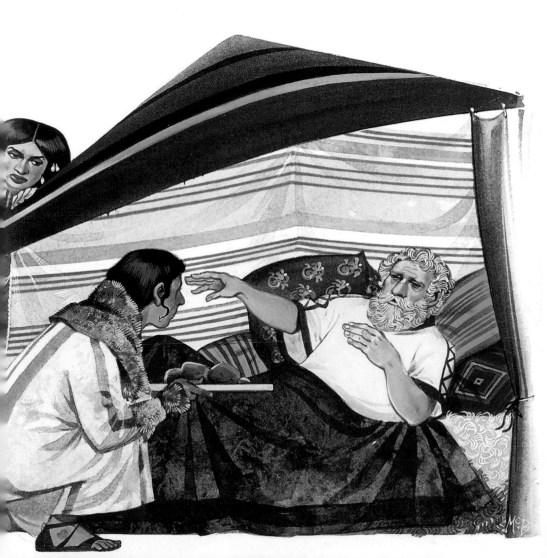

11. Jacob's Dream

Jacob is alone in the field. He cannot live
at home any longer. His brother, Esau,
is angry with him. He wants to hurt him.

It is dark and Jacob is very tired. He lies down on
the ground to sleep. He rests his head on a stone. He
uses it as a pillow.

Jacob dreams of **angels** climbing up the steps of a
ladder. He hears God say, "I will always be with you!"

This makes Jacob happy. He knows he is a child
of God. God will take care of him.

Genesis 28

God our Father, thank You that You are always with your children. Amen.

┌ **BOX**
CHAT *What are the angels doing? Where does Jacob rest his head? Point with your finger. Remember: God is with you, even when you are asleep or scared.*

12. Joseph Is Sold

Joseph is one of Jacob's twelve sons. Joseph's brothers do not like him. They say, "Our father loves Joseph more than he loves us!"

Jacob gives Joseph a beautiful coat. It makes his brothers very angry. They fight with him.

One day they grab Joseph and sell him to people who are traveling to a faraway land called Egypt. Poor Joseph!

But God takes care of Joseph. Joseph arrives safely in Egypt. He gets a good job.

Genesis 37

God our Father, thank You for taking care of me every day. Amen.

⌐BOX
CHAT
Can you see Joseph? Ask your mom or dad to give you some clothespins. Put eleven pins aside. One for each of Joseph's brothers. Add another peg for Joseph's one sister, Dinah. How many brothers and sisters do you have?

13. Joseph Is in Jail

Now Joseph is in Egypt. He works for a wealthy man named Potiphar. Joseph works hard. Soon Potiphar makes him head of his household.

But Potiphar's wife tells ugly lies about Joseph, and poor Joseph is thrown into jail. There, God helps him by making everyone in jail like Joseph.

Two men have strange dreams. They come to Joseph. God helps Joseph to tell them exactly what their dreams mean. Joseph tells them, "Do not forget me when you leave jail." One man promises to tell the king about Joseph.

When the men leave jail Joseph is alone again. But God has not forgotten him.

Genesis 39-40

God our Father, thank You for never forgetting me.
Amen.

CHAT BOX

Who will never forget you? God! And your mom and dad. Give each of them a big hug.

14. The King's Important Dream

Pharaoh is king of Egypt. He has a strange dream. Pharaoh says, "I see seven fat cows. And seven skinny cows eat them up. But the skinny cows stay skinny! What does it mean?" Nobody knows. Then suddenly one man remembers Joseph.

Joseph is taken out of jail to help. Joseph says, "God has sent this dream. There will be seven good years. Then there will be seven bad years.

Pharaoh must store away some food. Then the people will have food in the bad years." Pharaoh says, "I want you to work for me."

Joseph is happy. God has looked after him well.

Genesis 41

God our Father, thank You for knowing everything.
Amen.

CHAT BOX

*Put your thumb on the **seven** fat cows. Point with your little finger to the **seven** skinny cows. Where is Joseph? Where is Pharaoh?*

15. Joseph Sees His Brothers Again

Joseph is now an important man in Egypt. He makes sure that enough food is put away. Hungry people come from everywhere to buy food from him.

Then ten men arrive to buy food. Joseph immediately sees that they are his brothers.

But they do not recognize him!

Joseph's brothers treated him badly. Do you remember? But Joseph is kind to his brothers.

He gives them food. He doesn't even ask them to pay for it.

Genesis 42

God our Father, thank You that I can help people. Thank You for loving all people. Amen.

CHAT BOX

Do you see Joseph's brothers? God can use you to help other people, and even people who are not kind to you. Do you know someone you can help?

16. Joseph Forgives His Brothers

Joseph's brothers are back to buy food again. This time their youngest brother, Benjamin, is with them.

Joseph is very happy to see him. He gives each brother a bag of wheat. In Benjamin's bag he hides his best cup.

When they leave, Joseph sends people to catch them. They are scared!

But Joseph says, "I am Joseph, your brother. I forgive you." He is not angry with them.

Joseph sends his brothers to go get their father, Jacob. At last the whole family is together again.

Genesis 42–46

God our Father, thank You for always making sure that everything works out best for me. Amen.

⌐BOX
CHAT *What is in the bag? What is your best toy? How many donkeys do you see? Look carefully: one is hiding.*

17. Moses in the Basket

Moses is a baby. His mother and his sister, Miriam, are worried because Pharaoh wants to kill all the baby boys. They put Moses in a basket and hide him between the reeds at the river's edge. His sister, Miriam, hides in the bushes to keep an eye on him.

Pharaoh's daughter sees the baby in the basket. She feels sorry for him. Miriam comes closer and tells the princess, "I know a woman who can look after the baby."

So Mariam goes to get Moses' own mother! God takes care of Moses in this way.

Exodus 2

God our Father, thank You for giving me a mom and dad to take care of me. Amen.

Where is Moses, his mother, and sister? What else do you see? When it is time to take a bath, put a small plastic container in the water. Watch how it floats.

18. The Burning Thorn Bush

Moses is now a big, strong man. He leaves Egypt.
He looks after the sheep in the field.

One day he sees a fire. It is a burning thorn bush.
But something is strange: the leaves and branches are
not burning up. They are as green as ever.

Then God speaks, "Moses, take off your shoes. You are
not alone. I am God, and I have something I want you
to do! Go back to Egypt. I want you to help Me there."
In Egypt God makes Moses the leader of his people.

Exodus 3

God our Father, help me to listen when You talk to me. Amen.

⌐BOX
CHAT*Do you see how Moses listens to God? Today God talks to us through the Bible. Put your hand on the bush. Pretend it is burning. Ouch!*

19. God's People Leave Egypt

Pharaoh is the king of Egypt. He is making God's people work hard. God wants them to move out of Egypt. Moses tells Pharaoh what God has said. But Pharaoh says, "No! They stay!"

Then bad things start happening to Pharaoh and his people, the Egyptians, but not to the **Israelites**.

There are frogs everywhere. Then mosquitoes. Then hail so big that it kills people. Then darkness. Lots of terrible things happen. In the end Pharaoh listens. He says the people can now leave Egypt. God's people are very happy.

Exodus 6-13

God our Father, thank You for always protecting me.
Amen.

Why are there so many people walking?
*Did you know that **ten** bad things happened in Egypt?*
*Can you count to **ten**?*

20. God's People Walk Through the Sea

The **Israelites** are moving out of Egypt. They walk and walk until they come to a sea.

But Pharaoh has changed his mind. He sends his soldiers after them. The Israelites see the soldiers coming closer. They are frightened. They can't get through the sea.

But Moses tells them, "Don't be scared. God will do something wonderful!"

Then God makes a path through the sea. The people can walk through the sea. Their feet do not even get wet! Now they are safe. They sing because they are so happy.

Exodus 14

God our Father, thank You that because You love us You take good care of us. Amen.

CHAT BOX

Where is Moses? Where are Pharaoh's soldiers? Pretend that you are an Israelite. Let your fingers walk along the path through the sea.

21. God Makes the Water Taste Sweet

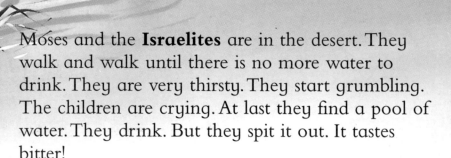

Moses and the **Israelites** are in the desert. They walk and walk until there is no more water to drink. They are very thirsty. They start grumbling. The children are crying. At last they find a pool of water. They drink. But they spit it out. It tastes bitter!

Moses says, "Don't worry, God will help." God tells Moses what to do. Moses throws a piece of wood into the water. The water becomes sweet! Everyone can now drink as much water as they want to.

Exodus 15

God our Father, there is no one like You. Thank You that
I can ask You to help me when I don't know what to do.
Amen.

Why are the people looking so unhappy? Put your
index finger on the piece of wood in the water. Look at
the circles it makes. God will always help His children.

22. God Gives His People Food

God's people, the **Israelites**, are in the desert.
They are very hungry. They get angry with
Moses. Moses says, "God will give us food to eat."
    The next day God sends them manna. Small white
flakes fall from the skies like rain. They scoop it up
with their hands and eat it. It tastes like bread.
God also sends birds called *quails*. The people catch the
birds in nets. Now they also have meat to eat.
God gives his people food.

Exodus 16

God our Father, thank You for giving us food and take care of us. Amen.

CHAT BOX

Look at the picture: Where are the birds, the quails? Where is the manna, the chunks of bread? What kinds of sweets do you like best? Pretend to eat manna with the children. Mmm…nice!

23. God Talks to His People

Moses and the **Israelites** walk a long way. They reach a big mountain. They decide to rest there. Moses climbs to the top of the mountain. There God talks to Moses. The storm on the mountain scares the people. God gives Moses ten rules. God writes them on two flat stones. The ten rules help God's people to love God and each other.

Moses reads the rules to the Israelites. They listen to what God says.

God our Father, please help me to always do what You ask me to do. Amen.

Look at the storm on the mountain. The people hear God's voice. In the church we call the ten rules the Ten Commandments *or God's Law.*

24.

The Ten Rules

1. There is only one God—God our Father.

2. God must be more important to you than anything else.

3. You should never forget who God is.

4. On Sundays you need to rest and go to church.

5. You should love your mom and dad. God wants you all to live happily together.

6. You may not kill or hurt anyone.

7. You must love the one you marry.

8. You may not steal anything.

9. You may not tell lies.

10. Be happy about who you are and about what you have.

Exodus 20

God our Father, please help me to love You and other people. Amen.

25. The People Make a Golden Calf

Where is Moses? He is talking to God on the mountain. Moses is taking a long time.

The people forget about God. They say to Aaron, Moses' brother, "We want a god that we can see."

Aaron says, "Bring your gold rings and bracelets."

Aaron melts them and makes a calf from the gold. Just then Moses comes down from the mountain! God is very angry with His people, because they have

forgotten Him so quickly. Moses pleads with God. God **forgives** His people. They promise to listen to God.

Exodus 24, 32

God our Father, thank You that You never stop loving us, even if we sometimes forget You. Amen.

CHAT BOX

Can you see the golden calf? Put a piece of paper over the calf so you can't see it anymore. Now the people are dancing and singing for God even though they cannot see Him. Remember: even though you cannot see God, He is always near you.

26. A Tent Where People Can Pray

God's people, the **Israelites,** have been walking through the desert for a long time. They live in tents.

God tells Moses to build a big tent. The tent is where the people can go to **worship** God. There, they can be close to God and praise Him.

They build a beautiful, big tent. It is the most beautiful tent of all. Everyone knows: here they can be with God. The tent is their church.

Exodus 25-26

God our Father, thank You that I can also go to church to be near You. Amen.

┌ **BOX**
CHAT *Point with your middle finger: where is the tent?*
Look: grown-ups and children are on their way to praise God!

27. Joshua and Caleb Tell About a Beautiful Country

The Israelites walk and walk. They come close to Canaan. God promised that they would live in this country. Moses sends Joshua, Caleb, and ten other men into the country.

Joshua and Caleb come back and tell everyone how beautiful it is. The other ten men say, "No, the people are too big and strong."

God's people are very scared of the giants. They have again forgotten that God can help them. This makes God very sad. He says, "Now you will have to stay in the desert."

The **Israelites** will only enter Canaan many, many years later.

Numbers 13-14

God our Father, thank You that when You are with us, we do not need to be frightened. Amen.

⌐**BOX**
CHAT *How do the grapes look? Pretend to eat some of them.*
Many years later God gave the country to His people, because He had promised it to them.

28. Rahab and the Red Rope

Moses climbs up a mountain. God takes him away. Moses is now with God. Joshua becomes the new leader of God's people, the **Israelites.**

God tells Joshua to send two men to the great city Jericho. In Jericho the two men look around to see what the city looks like. They have to be careful. The soldiers must not see them.

That night a woman named Rahab gives them a place to stay. But the soldiers see them! Rahab hangs a red rope from her window in the wall of the city. The two men climb down the rope quickly. They get away safely.

Joshua 2

God our Father, please help me to always help others. Amen.

┌BOX
CHAT Move your finger down the red rope to the bottom. The men tell Rahab she must hang the rope from her window again. If they see it, they will come to save her.

29. Everyone Walks Through the River

God's people are back again outside the country Canaan. God tells them they can now enter. But the Jordan River is full. The people ask, "How will we get through?"

Joshua says, "Wait, God will help us!"

Everyone has to walk in a long row. The **priests** walk into the water first. Then God makes a path through the river. Everyone can now walk through.

Joshua tells them to pick up twelve river stones. They place them in a pile. The pile of stones will help them to remember that God always helps!

Joshua 3-4

"God our Father, please help me to remember that You are always there to help. Amen.

CHAT BOX

Put one building block on another…and another one on top, like a pile of stones. The pile of stones helps everyone to remember that God helps His children!

30. The Walls of Jericho Fall

Jericho is a big city. There is a high, thick wall around the city. God's people want to get the people out of the city. God tells Joshua exactly what they must do.

For six days they walk around the city. On the seventh day they walk around the city seven times. Then the **priests** blow on their trumpets, and all God's people start shouting.

The thick walls come tumbling down. God's people enter Jericho.

Joshua 6

God our Father, thank You that no one is stronger than You are. Amen.

CHAT BOX *What is happening to the wall? Do you see the red rope? The Israelites remember to save Rahab and her family. Rahab is now one of God's people, too.*

31. God Helps Gideon to Be Brave

Gideon is afraid. He is hiding. Bad people, the Midianites, came to steal their food. They also stole all their sheep and cattle.

The Midianites do not know God. They worship a false god named Baal.

God comes to Gideon and says, "I will help you drive away the Midianites."

But Gideon answers, "Lord, please give me a sign that it is really You talking to me." Gideon then goes to kill a young goat. He puts the meat of the goat on a rock. Suddenly flames flare from the rock and burn the goat!

Now Gideon believes God. And God helps Gideon to be brave. Gideon and his men then leave to tear down the altar of Baal. God's people, the **Israelites**, now know that only God can help them.

Judges 6

God our Father, thank You that I can always talk to You because I am Your child. Amen.

┌BOX
│ *Ask mom or dad to help you draw a sad and fearful face.*
│ *Then draw the happy face of someone who is not afraid.*
CHAT
  God helped Gideon to be brave!

32. Ruth and Naomi Trust God

Naomi lives in a foreign country. Her husband and sons died. She is sad. She wants to return to her own country. Ruth was the wife of one of Naomi's sons.

Ruth goes back with Naomi. They are now living in Naomi's town called Bethlehem.

Naomi asks, "Where will we find food?"

Ruth says, "Naomi, God will help us."

Ruth meets Boaz. He is a rich farmer. He gives Ruth permission to pick up wheat on his farm.

Now Naomi and Ruth can bake bread to eat.

Later Boaz marries Ruth. They have a baby boy. Ruth is happy. She is now one of God's people, too.

Ruth 1-4

*God our Father, thank You for taking care of us every day.
Amen.*

*Where in the picture is Ruth? Where is Boaz? What is
Ruth doing? Pretend you are Ruth. Bend down and
pick up the wheat! Give it to your mom or dad.*

33. God Listens to Hannah

Hannah is unhappy. She has no children. The other women mock her. Hannah goes to the **temple**. She talks quietly to God. She asks God to please give her a child.

Not long afterward she has a baby boy. His name is Samuel. Now Hannah is very happy.

Samuel becomes a big boy. Hannah takes him to Eli, the **priest**. She promised God that she would bring Samuel to work for God. Samuel loves God very much.

1 Samuel 1-2

God our Father, please help me to always love You and talk to You. Amen.

CHAT BOX

Samuel's name means: I asked God to give him to me. *Ask your mom or dad what your name means.*

34. Samuel Hears a Voice

Samuel works for Eli in the temple. One night Samuel is fast asleep. Suddenly he wakes up. What is he hearing? A voice is calling, "Samuel!" He gets up and runs to Eli.

But Eli says, "I did not call you. Go back to bed and sleep."

A little later Samuel again hears a voice calling, "Samuel!" Then he hears the voice for a third time. Eli knows that it must be God who is calling Samuel. Eli tells Samuel to answer, "Speak, Lord, for I am listening."

From then on Samuel often talked to God.

1 Samuel 3

God our Father, please help me always to listen to what You teach me through the Bible. Amen.

┌─**BOX**
CHAT *Where is Eli? And Samuel? Remember: today God talks to us through the Bible. We call it God's Word. Close your eyes. Ask your mom or dad to read to you from their Bible: **Isaiah 41:13.***

35. Saul Becomes the First King

Samuel is now an old man. God's people come to
him. They say, "Samuel, you cannot lead us any
longer. Give us a king."

Samuel answers, "God is your king!"

But they say, "We want a king we can see."

God says that He will show Samuel whom to crown as king.

Who is that coming closer? It is Saul. He is searching for his father's donkeys. He is the tallest and most handsome of all the men. He becomes the king.

1 Samuel 8

God our Father, thank You that You are my King. It makes me very happy. Amen.

CHAT BOX

Point with your thumb: where is Samuel? Point with your middle finger: where is Saul? Pretend to be Saul. What will you say to Samuel?

36. God Chooses David

Now Saul is king of God's people. But he does not want to listen to God anymore.

God sends Samuel to the town of Bethlehem to choose a new king.

Samuel arrives at Jesse's home. God does not choose one of Jesse's seven tall, strong sons.

Samuel asks, "Do you have any other sons?"

Jesse sends for his youngest son, David. He is in the field looking after the sheep. Immediately God says to Samuel, "David is the one I choose."

1 Samuel 16

God our Father, thank You for wanting me to help You, too, even though I am still small. Amen.

⌐BOX
CHAT
What is David doing? Remember that to God you are special, too. Do your mom and dad have a special name for you?

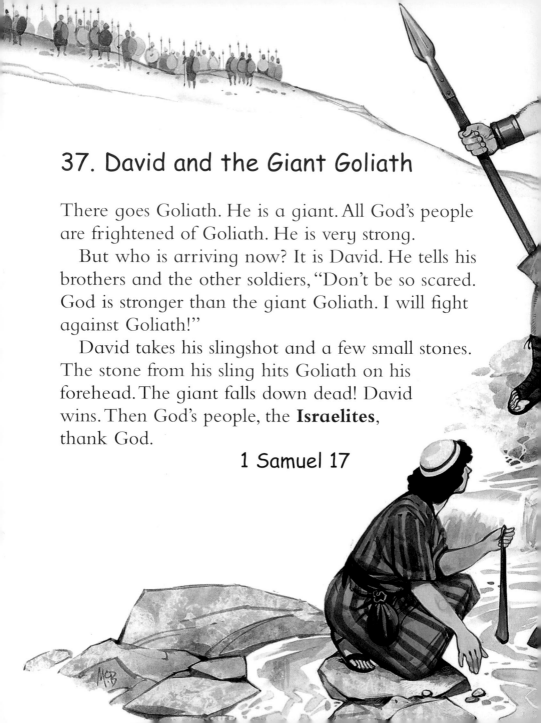

37. David and the Giant Goliath

There goes Goliath. He is a giant. All God's people
are frightened of Goliath. He is very strong.

But who is arriving now? It is David. He tells his
brothers and the other soldiers, "Don't be so scared.
God is stronger than the giant Goliath. I will fight
against Goliath!"

David takes his slingshot and a few small stones.
The stone from his sling hits Goliath on his
forehead. The giant falls down dead! David
wins. Then God's people, the **Israelites**,
thank God.

1 Samuel 17

God our Father, if You are with me, I don't need to be afraid. Amen.

⌐BOX
CHAT *Press with your hand on Goliath. Now point with your little finger: where is David? Who helped David to beat the giant Goliath? God our Father!*

38. Two Best Friends

David goes to live with King Saul. The **Israelites** all
like David. Saul is not happy about that at all.
Something beautiful happens. Saul's son, Jonathan, and
David become best friends. They do many things
together. They are good for each other.
Jonathan hears that his father, Saul, wants to kill
David. Jonathan is sad. He helps David to get away.
He shoots an arrow that travels a long way.
It is a sign to David that he must go far away.

1 Samuel 20

God our Father, thank You for giving us friends. Amen.

Who is your best friend? Where is David hiding? What is Jonathan shooting? Look, the boy is picking up the arrow.

39. David and Saul in the Cave

David and his men are in a cave. They are hiding from King Saul.

Saul comes along. He rests in the same cave! David creeps closer. What does he do? He cuts off a piece of Saul's clothes.

Saul gets up. David calls, "King Saul!" He shows Saul the piece of clothing.

Saul feels very bad. He sees that David is a good person. Saul says, "David, God is with you." He lets David go free.

1 Samuel 24

God our Father, please help me to always see good things in other people. Amen.

CHAT BOX

Where is David? Which one is Saul? Ask your mom or dad for a piece of cloth or paper. Cut a corner from it. This is what David did with Saul's clothes.

40. David Is a Good King

David has to live in another country. But he loves his people. He wants to go back to his country.

One day there is a big battle. King Saul and Jonathan are killed. David returns to his country. He becomes the king of God's people, Israel. King David asks if Jonathan has any children. He promised his best friend, Jonathan, that he would look after his children.

Jonathan's son Mephibosheth is brought to him. He cannot walk. Both his feet are crippled. David takes good care of him.

2 Samuel 9

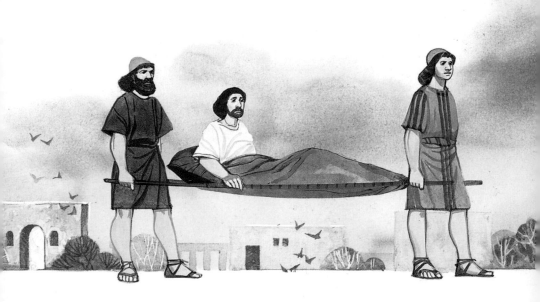

God our Father, please help me to always be kind to everyone. Amen.

CHAT ⌐**BOX**
└
Where is Mephibosheth? Do you know why he cannot walk? When he was a child someone dropped him. Do you know someone who is not well? Maybe you can visit that person and take him or her something.

41. Solomon's Wish

David grew very old and died.
Solomon is now the new king of
Israel. Solomon is David's son.
Just like his father, David,
Solomon also loves God.

   One night Solomon has a dream. He hears God
asking, "What do you want Me to give you?"
Solomon says, "I want to be a good king." God helps
Solomon. He makes him the wisest man in the world.

1 Kings 3

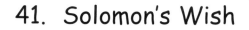

God our Father, thank You that You also help me to do good things. Amen.

What is Solomon doing in the picture? Yes, he is praying. You can also talk to God in the same way. God is with you. He wants to talk to you.

42. God Gives Elijah Food

Elijah is a **prophet.** He tells people about God. But there is a new king named Ahab. Ahab and his wife do not want to listen to God. Elijah scolds them. They get so angry that they want to kill Elijah. Elijah hides from them. But there is no food for him to eat. Elijah grows hungrier every day. What will happen to him?

God sends crows with meat and bread in their beaks. Now Elijah knows that God takes care of him.

1 Kings 17

God our Father, thank You that You know best what we need. Amen.

CHAT BOX

Can you tell which crows are bringing bread? And which crows are bringing meat? Think for a moment: how does God take care of you? By giving you a dad and a mom who can buy food. Ask if you can thank God for the food the next time you eat.

43. God Sets the Wood on Fire

God's people are struggling. There is no rain.
Elijah tells King Ahab and his people, "It is dry
because you no longer listen to God. You want
another god, Baal, to help you." Elijah puts wood
on two piles of stone. "Now ask Baal to make
your wood burn. I will ask God."

Nothing happens to their wood.

Elijah even pours water over his wood. God sets
the wet wood on Elijah's pile on fire! Baal's people
run away. Everyone now knows that God is
special. Baal is worth nothing. Then it starts raining.

1 Kings 18

*God our Father, You are very special to me. I love You
with all my heart. Amen.*

*Point with your index finger: where is Elijah? The Bible
calls such a heap of stones an **altar.** God's people bring a
bull or lamb as offering. They burn it on the altar. By doing
this they show that God is very special to them. Why is God
special to you?*

44. Elisha Helps a Poor Woman

A mother and her two sons live together. Their
father died, and they are very poor. What can she
do? She goes to Elisha to ask for help. Elisha tells
people about God. He is a **prophet**. Elisha tells the
woman, "Collect as many empty jars as you can. Pour
the little oil that you have in one of the jars."

God makes something wonderful happen. The jar
becomes full of oil! She pours oil into the other jars
until all of them are full. Now she can sell the oil.

God takes care of the mother and her sons.

2 Kings 4

God our Father, thank You for always helping me. Amen.

Where is Elisha? What is the woman doing? Press on the big jar. Now press on the small one. What does your mom bake with oil?

45. God Heals Naaman

Naaman is a soldier in a faraway country. A young girl works in his house. She loves God.

One day Naaman becomes very ill. The girl tells Naaman's wife about Elisha, the **prophet**. Elisha can make her husband well again.

Naaman takes her advice and visits Elisha. Elisha tells Naaman to wash himself in the river seven times. Naaman does it.

What happens? He is completely healed.
   From then on Naaman and his wife love God.

2 Kings 5

God our Father, thank You that You can make sick people
well. Amen.

⌐BOX
CHAT
What color is the wife's dress? And the girl's dress?
Remember: children can also tell other people about God.

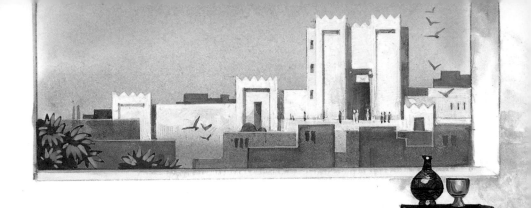

46. Hezekiah's Illness

Hezekiah is a king of God's people, the **Israelites.** He loves God very much. He also tells the Israelites to keep on loving God.

But then a terrible thing happens. Hezekiah becomes very ill. The doctors come. But they cannot help him at all. Hezekiah prays that God will make him well. God does so. Hezekiah is very glad. He keeps on thanking God.

2 Kings 20

God our Father, thank You for always listening to me when I pray. Amen.

CHAT BOX

Point to the sick Hezekiah. Pray right now and ask God to help the sick people. Are you healthy? Say: "thank You, God." Nod your head three times.

47. Josiah's Promise to God

Long ago everyone did not have a Bible, as we do today. There was only one book for all God's people. It was called the **Book of the Law**. But they forgot about it.

Then a new king was crowned—Josiah. He was only eight years old. He loved God with all his heart.

One day he asked the people to clean their church, the **temple**. The people found God's book. Josiah asked someone to read it to him. Then Josiah promised God that he and God's people would do as God told them in His book.

2 Kings 22-23

God our Father, thank You for telling me in the Bible what You want me to do. Amen.

┌BOX

CHAT *Do you enjoy listening to stories from the Bible? Choose one of the Bible stories yourself. Or do you want to hear this story again? Ask mom or dad to read you the one you have chosen.*

48. Jonah Doesn't Obey God

Jonah is a **prophet**. He must tell people about God. But Jonah doesn't want to obey God.

Jonah gets on a ship to run away from God. But God knows where Jonah is. God sends a storm. Jonah says to the people, "Throw me into the sea." They do so and the storm stops.

What happens to Jonah? God sends a big fish. The fish swallows Jonah. Inside the fish, Jonah tells God he is sorry. The fish spits Jonah out on the beach. Now Jonah will do what God asks.

Jonah 1-2

God our Father, help me to always do what You ask me to do.
Amen.

CHAT *What is Jonah doing? What is the fish doing? Can you*
swim? Use your arms to show how you swim.

49. Jonah and the Shady Tree

Jonah goes to Nineveh. It is a big city. Jonah tells the people not to do bad things. They tell God that they are sorry. But Jonah is unhappy. He does not like these people!

It is very hot. God makes a tree suddenly grow out of the ground. It keeps Jonah nice and cool. The next day the tree dies. Now Jonah complains. God says, "Just like you are sorry that the tree died, I feel sorry for the people and animals in the city."

God **forgives** the people of Nineveh. God gives
them another chance.

Jonah 3-4

God our Father, please help me to give people another chance.
Amen.

CHAT BOX
Point to the nice shady tree…and the dead tree…and Jonah.
Why did the tree die? An ugly worm made a hole in it.
Can you see the worm? Move your finger in a circle all the
way around the sun.

50. The Writing on the Wall

King Belshazzar loves parties. But he makes God very angry. He makes jokes about God.

Suddenly a hand appears and writes words on the wall. The king is afraid. His wise men cannot explain to him what the words mean.

They call Daniel. Daniel loves God. Daniel says, "God says that you will no longer be king."

That night another king captures King Belshazzar and all his people.

Daniel 5

God our Father, thank You for caring about your people. I love You with all my heart. Amen.

CHAT BOX
Do you see how frightened the king is? Where is Daniel? With your index finger draw a line underneath the strange words on the wall.

51. Daniel and the Lions

Daniel is an important man. He **prays** to God every day.

Some people do not like Daniel. They ask the king to make a new law. This law says people may not pray. But Daniel still prays. The bad people tell the king about it.

Daniel is thrown into a cage full of lions. The king likes Daniel and is worried. But God is with Daniel. The lions do not bite Daniel.

Now the king knows: Daniel's God is the real God. He tells all his people, "Always listen to God."

Daniel 6

God our Father, thank You that only You can save and help people. Amen.

52. God's People Return Home

God's people had to live in a faraway country, because they had stopped listening to God. So soldiers came and took them far away.

Now it is many years later. God tells them they must return to their own country. They go back to their old city, Jerusalem. But their hearts are sore. Their houses have been burnt down. And their beautiful church, the **temple**, as well. So they build a new temple, and they fix up their city.

God's people are now very happy. They promise God, "We will always listen to You."

Ezra 1, 5 and Nehemiah 8

God our Father, I promise to listen to You. Amen.

Where is the gate of the city? The people are on their way to the gate. How do they look? God's people are happy. Clap your hands to thank God with them.

New Testament

Jesus fulfills the promises God made to His people

We walk the road with our Lord Jesus, the Son of God.
We learn where Jesus was born and how He came to live
among the people. Jesus teaches us to be His helpers.
He helps us to love our heavenly Father
and to live happily with God forever.
We discover the secret
that Jesus is always in our hearts.

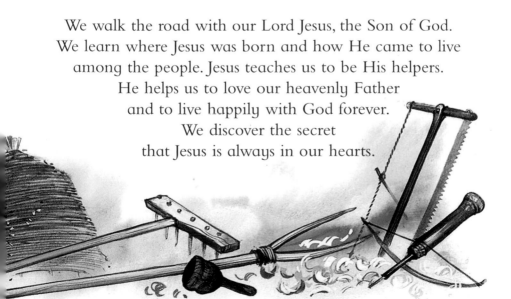

1. Mary and the Angel

Gabriel is a messenger from God, an **angel.** In a small town called Nazareth, he visits Mary. Mary is afraid! But the angel says, "Don't be scared."

He tells Mary she will have a very special baby. He says, "You must call your baby *Jesus*. He is the Son of God. He will save all the people who believe in Him."

Mary is glad and says to the angel, "I will do as the Lord asks."

Luke 1:26-38

*Our Lord Jesus, thank You for coming to save
everyone who believes in You. Amen.*

*What do you like best in the picture? Do you know
who is the most important in the whole world? Jesus!
The Bible tells us of Him. He loves you!*

2. The Baby Jesus

It is time for Baby Jesus to be born. Joseph the father and Mary the mother arrive in the town called Bethlehem. They search for a place to stay. But the town is full of people.

The only place they can find is in a stable where the animals sleep. Jesus is born in this stable. Mary, His mother, wraps Him warmly in cloths. She gently lays Him down on straw in a crib.

That evening was very special. God sent His Son to the earth.

Luke 2:1-7

Lord Jesus, we are so glad that You came to the earth. Amen.

CHAT BOX

Where is the Baby Jesus? Did you know that Jesus has a birthday? On Christmas day we remember Jesus' birth. Do you know a Christmas carol? Sing it on Jesus's birthday.

3. The Shepherds and the Angels

In the fields are men who look after the sheep. We call them shepherds. Suddenly they see a bright light.

An **angel** appears and says, "Don't be frightened. I bring you good news. Jesus was born. He has come to save people."

A choir of angels begins to sing beautifully.

The shepherds go to look for the baby. They are happy to find Mary and Joseph and Baby Jesus in the stable.

Luke 2:8–20

Lord Jesus, I am also happy, because I love You. Amen.

CHAT BOX
Point to the sheep, the shepherds, and the angels. Ask your mom or dad to shine a flashlight into a dark corner of the room. Do you see the shining light? That's how the angels appeared.

4. The Bad King

King Herod does not love God and treats people very badly.

One day wise men arrive to see the king. They come from a faraway country. They follow a bright star. This star is a sign that a great King was born. They ask King Herod, "Do you know where this King is?"

Herod wants to be the only king. He makes a plan. He is going to kill all the baby boys.

But God keeps Jesus safe. Jesus is the King of everyone who believes in Him.

Matthew 2:1–8

Lord Jesus, thank You that You are the great King of the world. Amen.

┌BOX
CHAT Point to King Herod and to the wise men.
They come from far away. How many
boxes do you see?

5. The Wise Men Find the Baby

The wise men are going to Bethlehem. They follow a bright star. The star stops above the stable where Jesus was born. They are very glad to find Mary, Joseph, and Baby Jesus there.

The men give Jesus their most beautiful gifts. Then they go back home.

An angel warns Joseph, "Beware! King Herod wants to kill the baby."

Joseph quickly leaves the town with Mary and Jesus.

They flee to another country called Egypt. When
Herod dies, they will return.

Matthew 2:1–23

Lord Jesus, please help me to always give You my best.
Amen.

CHAT BOX *Can you see Baby Jesus? Do you know the color*
of each of the wise men's coats?

6. The Boy Jesus Is Missing

Jesus grows up. He listens to His mother and father. He goes with Mary and Joseph to church, to the **temple** in Jerusalem.

Mary and Joseph are walking back home. Suddenly they notice Jesus is not with them! They turn back. Where is Jesus?

They find the boy Jesus in the temple. What is Jesus doing there?

He is talking to the clever men about God. God loves Jesus, because Jesus is God's Son.

Luke 2:41-52

Lord Jesus, I love You with all my heart. Amen.

CHAT BOX

What is Jesus doing in the picture? Can you see His mother Mary, and Joseph, His father? What are your mom and dad's names?

7. The Baby John

Zechariah and Elizabeth have no children. An angel comes to Zechariah. He says, "You will have a son."

But Zechariah does not believe him. He says he and Elizabeth are too old. He forgets that God can do anything. The angel tells Zechariah he won't be able to talk for a while.

The baby is born. Zechariah writes down the name John. It was the angel who told Zechariah to give the name John to the baby. Now Zechariah can talk again.

Luke 1:5-25, 57-66

Lord Jesus, thank you that You came to the earth to save all of us who believe in You. Amen.

┌BOX

CHAT

What is Zechariah writing? Do you see Elizabeth and the baby? Do you know what your name looks like in writing? Ask mom or dad to show you. Try to write it yourself.

8. John Baptizes the People

John is now a young man. God uses John to tell the people about Jesus. He also tells them to love God and **baptizes** them.

One day John is in the Jordan River. He tells the people that Jesus forgives those who are sorry for the wrong things they do.

Who is in the river with John? It is Jesus. John **baptizes** Jesus. Then God's voice from heaven says,

"This is My Son whom I love. Listen to Him!"

Matthew 3:1-17

Lord Jesus, help me to be obedient to You. Amen.

CHAT **BOX**
Point with your little finger to John. Point with your index finger to Jesus. God our Father also tells you, "You are my child, and I love you."

9. Jesus and the Devil

The **devil** does not want us to listen to God. The devil likes it when we do wrong things. It shows that we do not love God. It makes God sad. The Bible calls the wrong things we do **sin.**

The devil wants Jesus to do wrong things too. It will show that Jesus does not love God. But Jesus does not listen to the devil. Jesus says, "I only listen to God." Jesus is God's Son. The devil cannot harm Him. Then the devil leaves Jesus alone.

Matthew 4:1–11 and Luke 4:1–13

Lord Jesus, thank You for showing me how to listen to God and not to the devil. Amen.

How can we know what God wants? God tells us in the Bible what He wants us to do. Do you know what the desert looks like? It has more sand than the beach. There is no water. Nothing grows there.

10. Jesus and His Helpers

Simon

One day Peter and his brothers are catching fish. Jesus walks up to them and says, "Come, follow Me. You are going to help Me tell people about God. I will call you my **disciples**."

Jesus also called other people. They all followed Jesus.

Jesus' disciples were twelve special helpers. They loved Jesus and went everywhere with Him.

Mark 1:16-20 and Mark 3:13-19

Lord Jesus, thank You that I can also be your special helper. Amen.

┌**BOX**
CHAT *Ask mom or dad to read you the names of the disciples. Remember, a disciple is Jesus' special helper. If you love Jesus, you must listen to Him and help other people to learn about Jesus.*

Bartholomew

Philip

Thomas

Matthew

Thaddeus

Judas Iscariot

Andrew

James

Peter

James, son of Zebedee

John

Jesus

11. Jesus Helps a Lame Man to Walk

In Jerusalem there is a special pool. Many sick people are lying next to the pool. At certain times the water in the pool starts moving around. Then the sick people go into the pool to get well.

But next to the pool a man is lying who cannot walk. He is lame. He has no one to help him into the pool.

Who is coming? It is Jesus! Jesus says, "Get up and walk."

The man jumps up. He can walk! He thanks God for the miracle.

John 5:1-15

Lord Jesus, I pray for people who cannot walk. Won't You please help them? Amen.

CHAT BOX

Do you see the lame man and Jesus? Sit down and don't move. Count to five. Then jump up. Thank the Lord that you can jump and play.

12. Jesus Teaches Us to Pray

One day Jesus' helpers ask, "Jesus, teach us how to **pray.**"

Jesus teaches them patiently. He says, "God is your special Father. He loves you more than your own mom and dad. He looks after His children better than any mother and father. He only wants the best for you. Talk to your Father in heaven. He always listens when you pray."

Luke 11:1-4, 9-13

Lord Jesus, thank You for showing me how to talk to my special Father in heaven. Amen.

CHAT BOX

Praying is talking to God. God is your special Father. Do you also want to pray the prayer that Jesus taught His disciples? Ask mom or dad to read it to you in Matthew 6:9-13.

13. God Takes Care of Us

Jesus is sitting in a beautiful place. He talks to a large group of people. He points to the birds flying in the sky. Jesus says, "Do you see the birds? God our heavenly Father takes care of them. He gives them food to eat."

They see the birds. Jesus says, "Remember, God loves you even more. So, do not be worried. He will give you everything you need."

Matthew 6:25–34

God our special Father, thank You for giving us what we need. Amen.

CHAT BOX

Press with your thumb on the grass, flowers, tree, and birds. God cares for them. He takes even better care of you, because you are His child. Lift your thumb, and tell God how glad you are!

14. The Disciples Are Afraid

One day Jesus and His disciples are in a boat on the sea. Jesus is lying inside the boat, fast asleep. Suddenly a big storm comes up. The waves break over the boat! The disciples are getting very scared. They wake Jesus up. They need His help!

Jesus sees that they are very frightened. He tells the storm to be quiet and it stops! He says, "You do not have to be scared. I am with you."

Mark 4:35-41

Lord Jesus, thank You that when I am scared, I can know that You are always with me. Amen.

⌐BOX
CHAT *Press with your middle finger on the lightning. Name the things you are scared of. Remember, Jesus is with you. You are not alone.*

15. The Sick Little Girl

Jesus is talking to a group of people again. A man is pushing his way from the back through all the people. It is Jairus. He is looking for Jesus. He says, "My daughter is very sick. I know You can make her well."

Jesus goes with Jairus to his home. On the way someone comes running toward them. What is he saying? He is crying. He tells Jairus, "Your daughter is dead. You are too late."

Oh, no! But Jesus still goes to the house. He says to the girl, "Get up!" Immediately she is alive and well again. Everyone is happy.

Only God's power can do such wonderful things.

Mark 5:21-43

Lord Jesus, You are wonderful. I love You with all my heart. Amen.

CHAT BOX

What is the little girl in the picture doing? Where are her mom and dad? Remember, Jesus can really make people happy.

16. Jesus Feeds Many People

Many people have come to listen to Jesus again. It is getting late. The people are now very hungry. Andrew is one of Jesus' helpers. He says, "There is a boy here with two small fish and five loaves of bread. But it is not enough for all the people."

What can they do? Jesus takes the fish and the bread. He prays. Then He hands out the food. And guess what? There is more than enough food for everyone! Twelve baskets full of food are left over!

John 6:1-15

Lord Jesus, thank You for making wonderful things happen. Amen.

CHAT BOX
Where are the loaves of bread and the small fish? Why are all the people coming closer? Can you draw a fish? Ask mom or dad to help you.

17. Jesus Walks on Water

Jesus tells His **disciples,** "Take the boat across the lake." Jesus wants to be alone today. He wants to talk to God.

A strong wind starts blowing. The disciples row and row.

Who is out there? It is Jesus. He is coming toward them. Look! Jesus is walking on the water!

Jesus' helpers are very afraid. But Jesus says, "Don't be frightened. It is only Me!"

Jesus gets into the boat. And suddenly the wind stops blowing. The disciples look at one another. They know that Jesus is very special.

Mark 6:45-52

Lord Jesus, thank You for always being with me. Help me not to be frightened. Amen.

CHAT BOX

Can you draw a boat? Ask mom or dad to help you. Put the picture next to your bed. Look at it when you are scared. Remember, Jesus is always with you.

18. Jesus Heals a Deaf and Dumb Man

One day some people bring a man to Jesus. The man cannot hear or speak. He is deaf and dumb.

Jesus takes the man aside. He puts his fingers in the man's ears. Then He spits on His fingers and touches the man's tongue with His fingers.

First Jesus prays. Then He says, "Hear and speak again!"

Now the man can hear and speak. The people say to one another, "Jesus does good things."

Mark 7:31-37

Lord Jesus, thank You that everything You do is good. Amen.

┌BOX
CHAT *What is Jesus doing with the man? Put your finger on one of the people who are watching. Pretend that you are that person. What are you saying to the people around you?*

19. The Man Who Cared

Jesus tells a beautiful story. He says, "One day a man is walking alone along a dangerous road. Bad people beat him up. They steal all his possessions and leave. A **priest** comes by. But he doesn't want to help the man who is hurt. Someone else also comes along. But he, too, walks past. He is scared that the bad people may be somewhere near. He leaves the poor man lying there all by himself. Then a good man walks by. He cares. He stops to help the man. He puts the man on his donkey. He takes him to a house nearby."

That is how God wants us to care for others.

Luke 10:25-37

Lord Jesus, help me to be good to other people. Amen.

┌ **BOX**
CHAT *Do you see the two men who did not want to help?*
Where are the bad people hiding? What is the good
man doing? Remember, Jesus shows us how to care for
other people.

20. The Lost Sheep

Jesus teaches His disciples. He says, "I am like a good shepherd. A good shepherd knows the name of each of his sheep. The sheep know his voice. When he calls they come to him."

Then Jesus tells a story: "There was a shepherd who had many sheep.

One day one of his sheep got lost. Where could it be? The shepherd left the other sheep. He went to search for the lost sheep. When he found the lost sheep, he was very happy."

Jesus is like this shepherd. We are His sheep. Jesus cares for us very much.

John 10:1-15 and Luke 15:3-7

Lord Jesus, I'm sorry that I sometimes make You very sad. Thank You for caring so much about me. Amen.

CHAT BOX *Point with your little finger. Where is the sheep that was lost? If you could be one of the sheep in the picture, which one would you pick? Baa like a lamb that is very scared.*

21. The Son Who Ran Away

Jesus wants people to know that our heavenly Father loves us very much.

One day Jesus tells this story: "There was a good father who loved his two sons. But the youngest son ran away from home. After a while all his money was spent. He had to look after pigs! He felt very sorry that he had run away. He returned home to his father. His father was so glad to have him back home, that he had a big party."

Luke 15:11-24

Lord Jesus, thank You that I can know my heavenly
Father loves me very much. Amen.

CHAT BOX

How many pigs can you see? Why is the boy looking so unhappy? Close your eyes. What party was the best you ever had? Remember, your heavenly Father loves you.

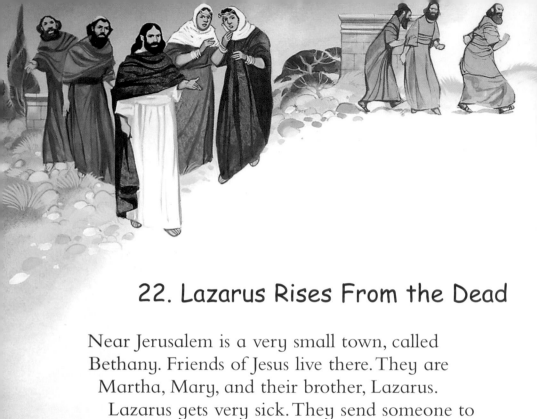

22. Lazarus Rises From the Dead

Near Jerusalem is a very small town, called
Bethany. Friends of Jesus live there. They are
Martha, Mary, and their brother, Lazarus.
Lazarus gets very sick. They send someone to
tell Jesus, "Come quickly!"

But Jesus is too late. Lazarus has already been dead for four days. But Jesus says, "You must believe that God can make him alive again."

Jesus goes with them to the grave. He calls in a loud voice, "Lazarus, come out!"

Lazarus walks out of the grave. He is alive again.

Everyone is very happy. They now believe that Jesus really is God's Son.

John 11:1-45

Lord Jesus, I believe that You can save people and make them happy. Amen.

Point to Jesus, Lazarus, Mary, and Martha. Do you know the colors of the people's clothes? Which color do you like best?

23. Ten Sick Men

One day Jesus is walking along a road. Ten men with ugly sores all over their bodies call out to Him, "Jesus, please heal us!"

Because of the sores they must stay outside the town. Nobody wants to come near them.

Jesus tells them to go into the town and show themselves to the **priests**.

While they are walking, their sores suddenly disappear.

One man turns round. He runs back to Jesus and says, "Thank You!"

The other nine men carry on walking away. They forget all about Jesus.

Luke 17:11-19

Lord Jesus, please help me to thank You for everything You do for me. Amen.

⌐BOX
CHAT *Do you see the man who has come back? What are some of the things you can thank Jesus for? Ask mom or dad to write it down. Put it in the back of the book. Take it out every now and then, and thank God again.*

24. Jesus Loves Children

One day a group of mothers bring their children to Jesus. His helpers, the **disciples,** scold the mothers, "Don't trouble Jesus."

But Jesus says, "Don't send the children away." Jesus loves children.

All the children run to Jesus. He hugs the children. He touches their hair. He says, "I tell you, children are very special to God."

Mark 10:13–16

Lord Jesus, thank You that as a child I am so special to You. Amen.

⌐BOX
CHAT
What do you see in the picture? Put your finger on one of the children. Pretend that you are that little child. What do you want to say to Jesus?

25. The Blind Man Can See Again

If you are blind, it means you can't see. Bartimaeus is blind. He cannot see the trees and the birds. He sits at the side of the road. He asks people who walk by to give him money.

One day he hears Jesus coming from afar. He begins to shout, "Jesus, help me!"

The people say, "No, keep quiet." But the blind man only shouts louder.

Jesus tells him to come closer. He helps him.

Now Bartimaeus can see. He is very happy.
He follows Jesus.

Mark 10:46–52

*Lord Jesus, please help blind people to know that You also
love them. Amen.*

CHAT BOX

*Let mom or dad tie a cloth over your eyes. How does
it feel to be blind? Today, blind people have dogs that can
help them. They also have a special Bible that they read
with their fingers. God takes care of blind people through
other people who help them.*

26. The Short Man

Zacchaeus is a short man. He is also very rich. But nobody likes him. People have to give him money for the king. But Zacchaeus takes some of the money for himself.

Zacchaeus hears Jesus is coming. He wants to see Jesus. He climbs in a tree.

Jesus sees Zacchaeus. He says, "Come down. I want to visit your home."

Jesus eats at Zacchaeus' home. Zacchaeus is very happy. From then on, he helps everyone and becomes one of Jesus' special **disciples.**

Luke 19:1-10

Lord Jesus, thank You for living in my heart and helping me to be good to other people. Amen.

27. Jesus Rides on a Donkey

Jesus and his **disciples** are getting close to the big city Jerusalem. Jesus asks two of them, "Go to the village and get a young donkey for me."

They find a donkey. A man, who is the owner of the donkey, asks, "Hey! What are you doing with my donkey?"

They say, "Jesus needs it."

Jesus rides on the donkey into Jerusalem. Many people stand along the sides of the street. They wave with palm leaves. They follow Jesus. They clap their hands. They shout, "The Lord is great! Here comes our King!"

Matthew 21:1–11

Lord Jesus, I know that there is nobody as great as You. Amen.

⌐BOX
CHAT

Look at the people's faces. What are they doing? They are laughing because they are happy that Jesus has come. Are you also happy that Jesus is with you? Clap your hands! Wave your arms!

28. Mary Shows Jesus Is Special

Jesus visits His friends. They are Martha, Mary, and Lazarus. Do you remember them? Jesus made Lazarus alive again.

Martha makes the food and serves the dinner. Mary takes an expensive perfume. She pours the perfume on Jesus' feet. Then she dries Jesus' feet with her hair.

The whole house smells nice. Why is Mary doing this? Jesus knows. She wants to show that Jesus is very special to her.

John 12:1-7

Lord Jesus, You are also special to me. Help me to show You how much I love You. Amen.

┌BOX

CHAT *Point to the bowl with the expensive perfume. Does your mom also have perfume? Ask her if you can smell it. Remember to tell Jesus every day that He is special to you.*

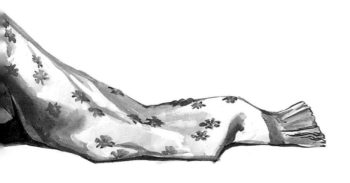

29. Jesus Gives Bad and Good News

Jesus talks with His special helpers, the disciples. He first tells them the bad news. He says there are people who do not like Him. They do not believe that He is God's Son. Jesus says they are going to kill Him.

The disciples are shocked to hear this bad news. Jesus knows that this bad news makes His disciples very sad. So He tells them the good news: "After three days

I will live again. Then I will go and live with God in heaven, and one day you will all come to live with Me."

Matthew 20:18–19 and John 14:1–3

Lord Jesus, thank You for loving us so much that You came to die for us. I love You, too, with all my heart. Amen.

┌ **BOX**

CHAT *What is Jesus doing? Who is listening to Him? It's His disciples. Jesus will also talk to you every day if you read the Bible. What did today's story tell you?*

30. The First Communion

Jesus and His disciples are eating together. Jesus breaks off a piece of bread for each one and says, "When you eat this, think of Me."

Jesus takes the cup with the wine. He says, "When you drink from this, remember that I gave my life for you."

Then Jesus looks at Judas. Jesus knows Judas is going to tell the soldiers where He is. The soldiers want to catch Jesus. Judas quickly gets up and walks out.

Jesus and the others finish eating. Then they sing together.

It is the first **Communion.**

Matthew 26:20-30

Lord Jesus, please help me to always remember what You did to save me. Amen.

CHAT BOX

Where is Jesus. Where is the bread and the wine? Do you see Judas? When you have Communion in your church remember to think of Jesus who died to save you.

31. The Soldiers Catch Jesus

The first Communion meal is over. Jesus and His disciples are walking in the beautiful Garden of Gethsemane. Who is coming?

It is Judas. Judas comes closer. He kisses Jesus. Now the soldiers know which of the men is Jesus. They catch Jesus.

Peter, one of the disciples, wants to help. He cuts off the ear of one of the soldiers. Ouch! Jesus touches the man's ear and makes it well. Then the soldiers take Jesus away.

The disciples are scared. But Jesus knows that He must give His life to save us.

John 18:1-11 and Luke 22:47-51

Lord Jesus, thank You for loving all people and wanting to help us. Please help people to believe in You. Amen.

CHAT BOX

Where is Jesus? Do you see Judas? Pick a leaf from a tree or draw a leaf on paper and cut it out. This leaf will remind you of what happened in the Garden of Gethsemane. Remember, Jesus wants to make people happy.

32. Jesus Hangs on a Cross

The soldiers have captured Jesus. Some people want to kill Him. They go to Pilate. Pilate is the most important man in that part of the country. Pilate says, "Jesus did nothing wrong."

But the people shout loudly, "Crucify Him!"

The soldiers put Jesus on a cross. Jesus suffers a lot of pain as He hangs there. Then Jesus prays. He asks God to **forgive** the people for hurting and killing Him.

In the middle of the day, it suddenly becomes dark. Jesus died!

One of the soldiers says, "He really is the Son of God!"

Matthew 27:11–55

Lord Jesus, thank You for suffering so much pain, so
that God can forgive me if I'm really sorry about the
things I do wrong. Amen.

┌BOX
CHAT Do you see Jesus on the cross? Make a paper cross and
color it. Ask mom or dad to help you. Hang the cross
in your room. Remember every time you look at it that
you are God's child.

33. Jesus Is Alive Again!

Jesus died. On Friday the people buried Him in a beautiful garden.

Early the next Sunday morning a woman goes to the grave. Her name is Mary Magdalene. What does she see? The grave is empty. She begins to cry.

Suddenly two **angels** in white clothes appear before her. They ask, "Why are you crying?"

She says, "Jesus is gone!"

Then a voice calls behind her, "Mary!"

It sounds like Jesus' voice. Mary turns round and looks. Yes, it really is Jesus. He is alive! She runs quickly to tell the others the good news: Jesus is alive!

John 20:1-10

Lord Jesus, thank You that You are alive and that if I believe in You, I can be part of God's family forever. Amen.

┌BOX
CHAT *Do you know someone who is called Magda or Dalene? Their names might come from Mary Magdalene in the Bible? She was the first to see Jesus alive again.*

34. Two Men on the Road

Two friends of Jesus are walking along the road.
They wonder about Jesus. Some say He is alive
again. Is He really dead?

A stranger comes along and walks with them.
He says, "The Old Testament tells us how the Son
of God will save those who believe in Him."

When they reached the
little village called
Emmaus, they say,
"Stay and eat
with us."

The stranger
breaks the bread
and gives them
each a piece.
Then they see that
it is Jesus! Suddenly
Jesus disappears.

The men quickly run to tell the disciples, "Jesus is really alive! We saw Him with our own eyes!"

Luke 24:13-35

Lord Jesus, I know that You are alive. Thank you that the Bible tells me so. Amen.

CHAT BOX

Where is Jesus? How many birds can you see flying? Can you draw birds that are flying? Ask mom or dad to help you.

35. The Friends Eat Fish

Peter and some of Jesus' other friends are in a boat. They are trying to catch fish. But all night they catch nothing.

In the morning they see a man standing on the beach. He says to them, "Throw your nets out again!" This time they catch fish. Then they know that it is Jesus!

They get to the beach. Jesus is grilling some fish. They eat fish and bread for breakfast. Then Jesus disappears again. They quickly ran to tell the others, "Jesus is alive!"

John 21:1-14

Lord Jesus, thank You for being good to me also. I am so happy that You are alive. Amen.

How many little fish can you see? Ask dad or mom if you can also have a nice fish grill. Then you can think of Jesus who is alive.

36. Jesus Returns to His Father in Heaven

Jesus' friends, the **disciples,** are very happy. They have Jesus with them again.

But one day Jesus says, "I must now go back to my Father in heaven."

They climb up a mountain. A cloud appears. Jesus goes away in the cloud. The disciples stare up into the sky.

But then two **angels** in white clothes appear next to them. They say, "Remember, Jesus will come back one day. Then He will stay with you forever."

Acts 1:1–11

Lord Jesus, I know that You are now with Your heavenly Father. The Bible tells me so. Amen.

⌐BOX
CHAT *What is happening to Jesus in the picture? Jesus is now with God, His Father. We cannot see Him, but He can see us. He can see you. What do you want to say to Jesus today?*

37. The Holy Spirit Helps Us

After Jesus had left in the cloud, his **disciples** felt very sad. But before He left, Jesus promised, "You will not be left behind all on your own. I will send the **Holy Spirit** to live in you. He will help you to do your best for Me."

Now the disciples are waiting in a room. They are praying. Suddenly there is a noise like the blowing of a strong wind.

A flame comes to rest above each person's head. But the flames do not burn them. What can this mean? The Holy Spirit has come!

Acts 2:1–47

Lord Jesus, thank You for the Holy Spirit who helps me to do what You want me to do. Amen.

CHAT BOX *When dad or mom makes a fire again, have a look at the flames. Then think of the Holy Spirit. The Bible says the Holy Spirit lives in your heart.*

38. A Lame Man Walks Again

One day Peter and John go to their church, the **temple.** At the steps they see a man. He cannot walk. He was born a cripple.

The man asks, "Won't you please give me money?"

Peter says, "We do not have money. But Jesus lives in us. In the name of Jesus, get up and walk!" The man

gets up. He can walk! He is very glad. He dances. He thanks God over and over!

Acts 3:1–10

Lord Jesus, thank You living in the hearts of your friends. Thank you that through the Holy Spirit You help us to help other people. Amen.

⌐BOX
CHAT *Press with your thumb on the crippled man. Why is he skipping and dancing? Can you dance? Ask mom or dad to help you spin round and round. Thank the Lord Jesus that you are healthy.*

39. Philip and the Man From Africa

Philip is one of Jesus' friends. He loves Jesus very much. Everywhere he goes, he tells people about Jesus.

One day an angel tells Philip to walk along a certain road. There Philip sees a wagon with a roof over it! A man is sitting in the wagon. He comes from Ethiopia in Africa.

Philip hears the man reading from the Book of Isaiah in the Old Testament. Isaiah said something about Jesus. The man does not know who Jesus is. Philip tells him the good news about Jesus, who loves us and saves us.

The man says, "I also want to love Jesus and do what He wants."

So the man from Africa became one of God's children, too.

Acts 8:26-40

Lord Jesus, please help me to tell other people the good news about You. Amen.

CHAT BOX
Where is Philip? Do you see the man from Africa? Ask dad or mom to show you on a map where Ethiopia is.

40. Paul Begins to Love Jesus

At first Paul was not a friend of Jesus. He arrested Jesus' friends, and threw them into jail.

Paul is on his way to a big city called Damascus. Suddenly he sees a bright light. It frightens Paul. He falls to the ground.

Suddenly he cannot see a thing. But he is hearing something. It is a voice. Jesus' voice! Jesus says, "I want to be your friend. From now on you will be My helper."

Only then did Paul start loving Jesus. He told everyone about Jesus.

Acts 9:1-19

Lord Jesus, thank You that I can be your friend. Help me to tell other people about You. Amen.

┌BOX
CHAT *Where is Paul? Can Paul see Jesus? Let mom or dad show you how to draw a beam of bright light. Color it yellow.*

41. Paul Escapes in a Basket

Paul now loves Jesus. He tells people that Jesus also loves them and wants them to stop doing wrong things. Some people do not like Jesus. They want to catch Paul and kill him. Watch out Paul!

But Jesus' friends hear about the danger. They take a big basket. Paul climbs into the basket. They lower the basket on the outside of the city wall.

Now Paul is safe. Paul can travel further. Everywhere he tells people about Jesus.

Acts 9:20–25

Lord Jesus, thank You for always helping your children. Amen.

CHAT BOX

Look how big the basket is! Paul can fit in it. Can you see that it is nighttime? What big bird woke up and is flying off? What sound does it make?

42. Peter Walks Out of Jail

Peter is telling people about Jesus. Many people do not want to believe in Jesus.

They catch Peter and throw him in jail. Peter is not at all scared. Jesus is with him. His friends are praying for him.

Suddenly an **angel** appears. "Come with me," he says.

The chains fall off Peter's hands and feet. The soldiers are fast asleep! The prison doors open by themselves. Peter quickly goes to Jesus' other friends. They are still praying. Then they hear someone at the door. It is Peter!

"Thank You, Jesus," they say.

Acts 12:1-19

Lord Jesus, thank You that I do not have to be scared. Thank You for listening to our prayers. Amen.

⌐BOX
CHAT *What is Peter looking at? Do you see the cuffs that are open? Ask mom or dad to cut from paper two half circles like imaginary handcuffs and put them on you.*

43. Timothy Helps Paul

When Timothy was a little boy, his granny and his mom told him about the Lord Jesus. Now Timothy is a young man. He has read a lot about the Lord Jesus. He wants to work for Jesus.

One day Paul arrives in his town. Timothy asks, "Paul, can I help you?" Paul needs a helper. Timothy goes with Paul.

Together they go to other countries to tell the people about Jesus.

Acts 16:1-5 and 2 Timothy 1, 3

Lord Jesus, I love You. I also want to tell others about You. Please show me how. Amen.

CHAT BOX
Where is Timothy, his mom, and his granny?
Can you purr like a cat? What else do you see in the picture?

44. Paul and Silas Are in Jail

Paul and Silas tell people about Jesus. The people in the city Philippi do not want to hear about Jesus. They throw Paul and Silas in jail.

In the jail the two men sing songs to praise the Lord. Suddenly the ground shakes. The doors of the jail swing wide open!

The guard at the jail is afraid. But Paul and Silas do not run away. They say, "Come, let us tell you about Jesus."

The guard learns to love Jesus. They all thank God.

Acts 16:16–40

Lord Jesus, thank You that You want all the people to know You. Amen.

We sing songs to Jesus to thank Him. Ask mom or dad to teach you a song. Which song can you now sing for Jesus?

45. Paul and the Terrible Storm

Where is Paul? He has been caught again by the
people who do not love Jesus. They put him on a ship.
Paul must go to the big city of Rome. There he must
talk to the king.

A big storm comes up. The people on the ship are
very scared. They think they are going to drown.

Paul says, "Don't worry! I am God's child. Nobody
will drown. God will take care of us."

The sea pushes the ship onto a sandbar. Phew! The
people swim safely to the beach just as God promised.

Acts 27

Lord Jesus, thank You for taking such good care of Your children. Amen.

⌐BOX
CHAT *Which one is Paul? How many other men can you count? Pretend you are Paul. What do you say to the other men?*

46. Onesimus Runs Away

Onesimus works for Philemon. Philemon is a very rich man.

But one day Onesimus decides to run away. He is caught and thrown into jail. Who is also there in the jail? Look, it is Paul!

Paul tells Onesimus about Jesus. Onesimus becomes a child of God.

When Onesimus gets out of jail, Paul tells him to go back to Philemon.

Paul writes a letter to Philemon while he is in jail. He writes, "Onesimus now knows the Lord. Take him back. Love him. He is a dear brother to me."

Philemon took Onesimus back again. They were both children of God. Philemon and Onesimus lived happily together.

Philemon

Lord Jesus, please help me always to give my best to other people. Amen.

⌈**BOX**
CHAT *What is Paul doing? The letter he is busy writing can be found in the Bible. Ask mom or dad to show you Paul's letter to Philemon. You'll see. It's a short letter.*

47. Jesus' Big Family on Earth

Jesus' friends are telling everyone about Jesus. They also decide, "Every Sunday we are going to get together. That way we will remember that Jesus is alive."

They talk to each other about Jesus. They also sing and pray and eat together. They love Jesus. They remember that Jesus said, "If you love Me, you must love others too." They also care for each other.

If anyone needs anything, they all help.

More and more people join them. They are like one big family. We call it a *church*.

Acts 2:43–47

Lord Jesus, thank You that I can also be part of Your church. Amen.

How many little children do you see in the picture? Are you happy to be part of the congregation in your church? Sing your favorite song for Jesus.

48. Jesus Comes Again!

Jesus is not on earth anymore. He now lives with God, where we cannot see Him. One day Jesus will come back to earth. He promised this to His friends.

Then we will be able to see Jesus again. Then Jesus will make everything on earth very beautiful. All God's children will be happy. Nobody will get hurt any more. Nobody will cry any more.

The most wonderful thing is that Jesus will live with us forever. Does that make you happy?

Revelation 21:1–27

Lord Jesus, thank You that if You promise something, we can trust You to do it. Amen.

┌BOX
CHAT *What are the people in the picture doing? What is the prettiest thing in the picture for you? The Bible says not even the most beautiful picture can show us how it will be when we stay forever with the Lord Jesus.*

Difficult Words Explained to the Little Ones

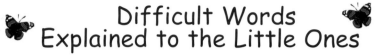

Devil: He wants to spoil all the beautiful things that God has made. He does not love God. He also does not love people who love God. He wants them to be disobedient to God.

Israelites: They are God's people. They love God. They live in the country God has promised them. They must tell other people about God.

Worship: All God's people come together to be with God. They sing songs to praise Him and talk to Him.

Pray: It is to be quiet in God's presence and to talk to Him. You can talk to God wherever you are.

Priests: They were specially chosen to teach God's people how to worship Him. They were the parsons of His people.

Temple: It is the place where God's children went to when they wanted to be alone with God and speak to Him. It was their church.

Prophet: A man or woman that has to tell God's people what He said. They must also tell other people about God, so that those people too will love God.

The Law of God: A special book in which God tells His people what they must do if they want to live close to Him.

Forgive: God forgets the things we did that hurt Him. God always gives us another chance.

Angel: An angel is not a human being like you and me. Angels are the messengers of God. The Bible tells us that angels dressed in white clothes visit people to tell them what God has said and what God wants them to do.

Baptize: When you are baptized with water in your church, you prove that you are God's child and that you know He loves you very much.

Sin: We sin when we do not listen to God. We only think of the things that *we* want to have. We don't even care if we hurt God.

Disciples: They are Jesus' special helpers. They have to tell people that God loves them. You are also a disciple because you love Jesus and tell other people about Him.

Communion: It is when we remember Jesus' last supper with his disciples before He died on the cross. Jesus died to save us. We also remember that He has risen from the dead. He is always with us, even though we cannot see Him.

The Holy Spirit: Jesus promised His helpers, His disciples, that we would never be alone. God sent His Holy Spirit to live in your heart. The Holy Spirit helps you to give your best to God.

The Little Children
and Jesus

People were bringing little children to
Jesus to have Him touch them, but the
disciples rebuked them. When Jesus saw
this, He was indignant. He said to them,
"Let the little children come to Me, and
do not hinder them, for the kingdom of
God belongs to such as these. I tell you
the truth, anyone who will not receive the
kingdom of God like a little child will
never enter it." And He took the children
in His arms, put His hands on them
and blessed them.

Mark 10:13–16

The Illustrations

The illustrator, Angus McBride, has taken great pains to provide illustrations that are both biblically and historically correct and speak to the world of the young child. He has, for example, clothed the various biblical characters in the same clothes, so that they may be easily recognizable for a child. Moses always wears an overcoat with black, red and white stripes. These are the colors of the people of Levi. David's is blue with dark blue stripes, and Rebecca's blue with pale blue stripes.

According to the Table of Esachila, a hieroglyphic document dated 229 B.C. which is kept in the Louvre in Paris, the Tower of Babel consisted of terraces. It was roughly 295 feet high and stairs led to the top story. On the highest terrace was a shrine from which the divinity could descend to the people by means of the stairs. In those days such a tower would function as an elegation for a temple.

Joseph's brothers are wearing the colors that would eventually be symbolic of each Israelite clan. Reuben, for instance, is wearing red; Simeon green; Judah blue and white; Issachar black; Zebulon a pale grey; Gad cream; Dan purple, and so on.

It is very difficult to portray Satan, as he has no human image. Nobody knows what he looked like. So the artist has given his own interpretation of Satan in the temptation story, as a shadow against a rock.

The twelve disciples are portrayed and all their names given. In all the stories the disciples will be wearing the same clothes, so that they may be easily recognizable.

These are just some of the incredible thought processes that went into the creation of the wonderful illustrations in this book. May each child and parent be touched and blessed by them!